SO! WORKS IT OUT

Written by Joanna Nadin
Illustrated by Daniel Duncan

This book is about idioms. An **idiom** is a phrase or group of words which together have a special meaning that is not obvious from the words. For example, 'I could eat a horse!' means 'I'm hungry!'

OXFORD
UNIVERSITY PRESS

Words to look out for ...

alter (verb)
alters, altering, altered
To alter something is to change it.

alternative (adjective)
something you can choose instead of something else

conceal (verb)
conceals, concealing, concealed
to hide something or keep it secret

concept (noun)
an important general idea

ensure (verb)
ensures, ensuring, ensured
To ensure that something happens is to make sure of it.

establish (verb)
establishes, establishing, established
To establish a fact is to discover if it is true, or show that it is true.

process (noun)
a series of actions or events that cause something to happen

methodical (adjective)
careful, and logical or well-organized

Chapter 1

Sonny loved most things about his nana and grandpa.

He loved their house full of cool old things. He loved their habit of having biscuits as a snack every morning. He also loved their cat, Cardboard. This was lucky, because he often stayed with them when his parents were working.

There was one thing he didn't love, though. He didn't love the confusing way they spoke.

It was because they used phrases that just didn't make sense to him.

When they sat down for a cup of tea and a biscuit, they called it elevenses. It was never at eleven o'clock though! It was at different times in the morning, depending on how they felt. Sonny often found it hard to know what they were talking about.

One Saturday, Sonny's parents had to work, so Mum dropped Sonny off at Nana and Grandpa's.

'Have fun!' she called as she left.

'We will!' promised Grandpa. 'As sure as eggs is eggs!'

Sonny thought this was a very strange thing to say. What did eggs have to do with anything? Their odd way of talking had started already. He couldn't conceal his disappointment.

To conceal something is to hide it or keep it secret.

'Why the long face?' asked Grandpa, once Sonny had hung up his coat.

He was speaking oddly again! Sonny knew that it was better to ask questions when you didn't understand something than to stay quiet.

'I don't know what you mean,' Sonny admitted. 'My face isn't long.'

Grandpa frowned. 'I see,' he said. 'Well, long face just means you look sad.'

It was Sonny's turn to frown.

Grandpa smiled. 'You alter the words you use to say something ... but in a different way. It's a sort of code,' he explained.

Sonny thought. A code? He quite liked cracking codes. It was a difficult process working them out, but fun when you finally understood them.

'Why long face though?' Sonny asked.

To alter something is to change it.
A process is a series of actions or events that cause something to happen.

Grandpa took Sonny to a mirror. 'Look at your face when you smile,' he said.

Sonny did as he was told. He smiled into the mirror. His face got a bit shorter!

'Now try to look sad,' said Grandpa.

Sonny stared sadly into the mirror. 'Wow!' he said. 'My face does look a bit longer.'

'Idioms are different ways of saying ordinary things. It seems an odd concept but it can be fun, too,' explained Grandpa.

Sonny wasn't sure it was fun. He preferred it when people said what they meant. 'I think I get the idea,' Sonny said.

'Now, let's find Nana,' said Grandpa. 'Be careful, though. She got out of the wrong side of the bed this morning.'

A concept is an important general idea.

'Did she?' Sonny said, scratching his head. 'Which is the wrong side?'

'It's another idiom,' chuckled Grandpa. 'It means she woke up feeling grumpy.'

Sonny thought about it. Well, he would be grumpy if he'd got out of the wrong side of his bed, too. Especially if he bumped into the wall.

Pleased with himself for understanding, he smiled and followed Grandpa into the front room.

Grandpa was right, Nana had got out of the wrong side of bed. She had a cup of tea and a biscuit, which were her favourites. Even after those, she still seemed cross.

Sonny looked over at Grandpa, who smiled gently back.

Nana sighed. 'Sorry, Sonny. Unfortunately, my glass is half empty today,' she said.

Sonny was confused again.
Nana had a cup, not a glass.

Grandpa handed Sonny some orange juice. 'Look at your glass of orange juice,' said Grandpa.

'Now, let's establish whether it's half full or half empty,' said Grandpa.

Sonny frowned. Was this a trick? 'Half full?' he asked, unsure. It was both half full and half empty, wasn't it?

To establish a fact is to discover if it is true, or show that it is true.

'Aha! If you're the kind of person who sees the positive side of things, you'd say the glass was half full because you're happy with what you have,' explained Grandpa.

Sonny nodded.

Grandpa continued. 'If you're the kind of person who sees the gloomy side of things, you'd say it was half empty. You'd be sad about what you *don't* have,' he said.

It was a lot to take in, but Sonny thought he understood. 'So, it depends on how you look at the glass,' he said.

'Exactly,' said Nana. 'I'm certainly not wearing my rose-tinted glasses today. Everything's a bit gloomy.'

'Where are your glasses?' asked Sonny, though he couldn't remember Nana ever wearing any glasses at all.

Nana flung up her hands. 'I must have lost them.'

'I'll help you look!' offered Sonny.

Grandpa had other ideas. 'How about we all go to the park?' he suggested. 'Fresh air always cheers me up.'

'It's chilly outside,' said Nana.

Sonny thought hard. 'You can wear your new coat,' he said.

'I suppose so,' sighed Nana.

Grandpa grinned. 'Well done, Sonny,' he whispered. 'That was real glass half full thinking.'

Chapter 2

They all walked to the park.

'Shall we give the slide a spin?' asked Grandpa.

'Don't you mean the roundabout?' asked Sonny.

'Ah, sorry Sonny,' said Grandpa. 'That's another idiom! Give it a spin means to give it a try.'

Sonny wondered again why adults didn't just say what they meant. It would save a lot of time! He smiled anyway. He liked the slide.

'Let's give the slide a spin,' said Sonny. 'Then we can do the same with the roundabout.'

'Well done,' Grandpa said. 'You've got it!'

Sonny climbed up the slide to give it a spin.

He and Grandpa went first.

'Keep your legs straight,' Grandpa told him. 'Then lean back to ensure you go faster!'

To ensure that something happens is to make sure of it.

Sonny whooshed down the slide first, followed by Grandpa.

'That was amazing!' Sonny yelled.

'The best thing since sliced bread!' agreed Grandpa. 'That means the same as "amazing".'

Sonny had a good think about sliced bread. Whenever Dad tried to cut slices from a whole loaf, it ended up in thick chunks. Already-sliced bread really was amazing!

'Your turn now, Nana,' said Sonny.

'No, I don't think so,' she grumbled.

'Please?' begged Sonny. 'It really is the best thing since sliced bread!'

'Oh, all right,' said Nana. She plodded up the steps in a methodical way.

'Legs straight,' Sonny called up to her, when she finally got to the top.

'Now lean back,' added Grandpa.

'Go!' yelled Sonny.

Methodical means careful, and logical or well-organized.

19

Nana flew down the slide so fast that she landed with a thump.

'Are you OK?' Sonny asked.

Nana pulled herself up. 'I'm fine,' she said, brushing dust off her coat. 'I don't think it's as good as sliced bread though.'

'Not everyone likes the same thing,' thought Sonny.

'Maybe the roundabout's more your style?' said Grandpa.

'Maybe,' agreed Nana.

Sonny and Nana climbed on
to the roundabout. Grandpa spun them
until Sonny's head span as well.

'Stop!' cried Nana. 'I'm too dizzy!'

Grandpa stopped the roundabout
and Sonny happily staggered off.

'I think we bit off more than we
could chew with that one,' said Nana.
She had to sit down to stop herself
falling over.

Sonny thought hard. 'Does that mean we spun too much?' he asked.

'Yes! It means we took on more than we could cope with,' said Grandpa. 'It's an alternative way to say it.'

Sonny smiled, but then he glanced at Nana. She was looking a bit ill.

Then Sonny had an idea. 'The swings!' he said. 'You won't bite off too much with them!'

An alternative thing is something you can choose instead of something else.

First of all, Nana pushed Sonny. She pushed really hard and Sonny flew up higher and higher, until he thought he might be able to touch the sky.

'Brilliant!' Sonny yelled. 'Now it's your turn!'

Nana pulled a face as they swapped places.

Grandpa gave a smile.

'Maybe the swings will be more your cup of tea,' he said to her.

Sonny gave the swing a big push. He thought hard again. 'I guess your cup of tea means something that you like, right?' Sonny asked.

'That's right!' said Grandpa. 'The swings and the slide were your cup of tea, weren't they?'

Sonny nodded. 'Yes!' he said.

Nana gave a squeal of happiness.

'And I think the swing is Nana's cup of tea, too!' said Sonny.

'I felt like a little girl again!' said Nana, once she'd got off the swing.

'The best thing since sliced bread?' asked Sonny.

Nana grinned. 'Absolutely,' she said. 'In a sandwich with jam on! Thanks, Sonny.'

Sonny felt himself glow with happiness.

'Talking of sandwiches,' said Grandpa, 'We should get back for elevenses.'

Chapter 3

As they headed back, Sonny thought about the morning. He really had helped <u>alter</u> Nana's glass from half empty to half full. She'd found something that was the best thing since sliced bread, too! Then a sudden thought struck him. What if she woke up on the wrong side of the bed tomorrow? He would be back home and wouldn't be able to help. Unless ...

To <u>alter</u> something is to change it.

'What if I got her a present?'
Sonny thought. 'Presents always cheer people up.' He only had a pound, so it would need to be something small.

'Not flowers, then,' he thought as they passed the flower shop.

'Nor a vase,' he decided as they passed a gift shop.

Then, as they got to the charity shop, Sonny spotted something.

'Can I go in here?' he asked.

'Not for too long,' said Grandpa, 'I could eat a horse!'

For a moment, Sonny was worried. Then he thought about the words. Grandpa wouldn't really eat a horse, he was just really, really hungry! Sonny hurried into the shop and selected a present for Nana.

'What did you get?' asked Nana.

'Oh, you'll see,' said Sonny.

'Here's your elevenses,' said Grandpa, handing Sonny a fresh buttered scone.

Sonny checked the clock and laughed. It was closer to lunchtime, not eleven o'clock, but that didn't matter. He finally understood what Grandpa meant now.

After he'd finished his scone, he remembered the present. He hoped Nana was going to like it.

'Here you are,' said Sonny, handing Nana a small bag. 'I bought this for you in the charity shop earlier.'

Nana's face lit up with joy when she opened it. 'Rose-tinted glasses!' she laughed.

Sonny nodded happily. 'Don't you remember? You said you couldn't find yours earlier,' he said.

'Of course!' Nana laughed.

'But, Sonny, here's the thing ...' began Grandpa.

'I know, I know,' Sonny interrupted. 'It's an idiom. Looking at something through rose-tinted glasses means it makes gloomy things look better.'

Grandpa patted him on the back. 'Amazing,' he said. 'You're the King of Idioms now!'

'Am I really?' asked Sonny. Grandpa smiled and said, 'Well, no, not really, but ...'

'I know,' said Sonny. 'It just means I'm good at them!'

From then on, Sonny began to enjoy the way his grandparents spoke. He was no longer confused by what they said. Instead, he always tried to work out what the idioms really meant. It was a lot of fun trying to crack the code!

He also enjoyed elevenses whenever he liked.